STEM

Robots

3-D Shapes

Joseph Otterman

Consultants

Colene Van Brunt
Math Coach
Hillsborough County Public Schools

Publishing Credits

Rachelle Cracchiolo, M.S.Ed., *Publisher*
Conni Medina, M.A.Ed., *Managing Editor*
Dona Herweck Rice, *Series Developer*
Emily R. Smith, M.A.Ed., *Series Developer*
Diana Kenney, M.A.Ed., NBCT, *Content Director*
June Kikuchi, *Content Director*
Susan Daddis, M.A.Ed., *Editor*
Karen Malaska, M.Ed., *Editor*
Kevin Panter, *Senior Graphic Designer*

Image Credits: pp.8–17, p.19 Walter Mladina; all other images from iStock and/or Shutterstock.

Library of Congress Cataloging-in-Publication Data

Names: Otterman, Joseph, 1964- author.
Title: STEM. Robots / Joseph Otterman.
Description: Huntington Beach, CA : Teacher Created Materials, [2019] |
    Includes index. | Audience: Grades K to 3. |
Identifiers: LCCN 2017055073 (print) | LCCN 2018001003 (ebook) | ISBN
    9781480759879 (eBook) | ISBN 9781425856939 (pbk.)
Subjects: LCSH: Robotics--Juvenile literature.
Classification: LCC TJ211.2 (ebook) | LCC TJ211.2 .O858 2019 (print) | DDC
    629.8/92--dc23
LC record available at https://lccn.loc.gov/2017055073

Teacher Created Materials

5301 Oceanus Drive
Huntington Beach, CA 92649-1030
www.tcmpub.com

ISBN 978-1-4258-5693-9

Table of Contents

Robot Surprise

"We get to build robots?"

The class was not sure they had heard Miss Lopez correctly. Did she really say they would build robots? They hoped so. Building robots would be fun!

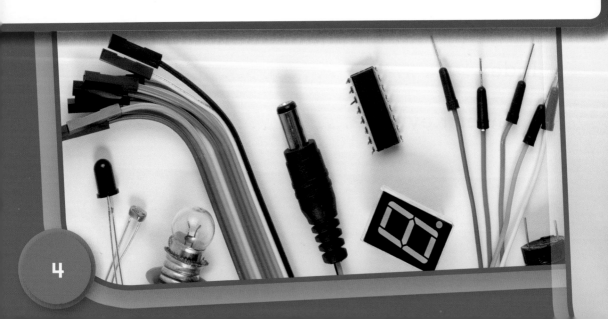

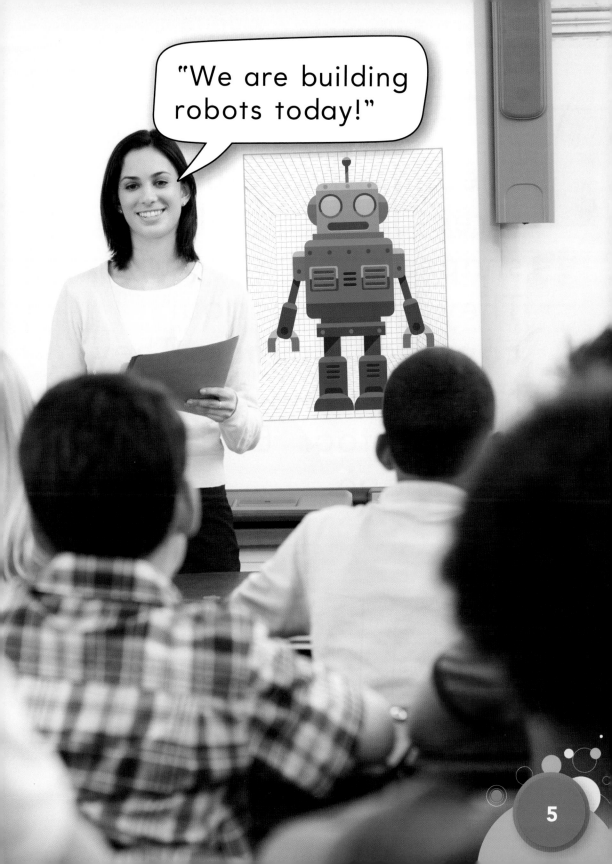

Shaping Up

The class had studied three-dimensional (3-D) shapes all week long. They learned about **cones** and **cubes**. They learned about other shapes, too. Each is a 3-D shape.

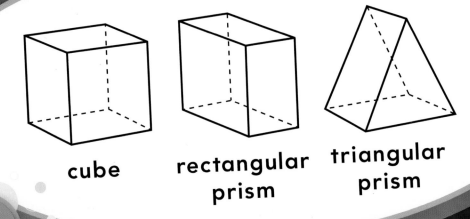

cube   rectangular prism   triangular prism

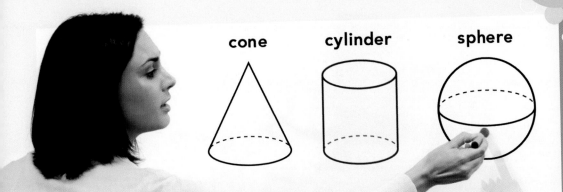

cone cylinder sphere

Miss Lopez plays a game with students. She gives them clues about 3-D shapes. Help students name the shapes.

1. I am a solid shape. I am round like a ball. What am I?

2. I am a solid shape. I have 6 **faces** that are squares. What am I?

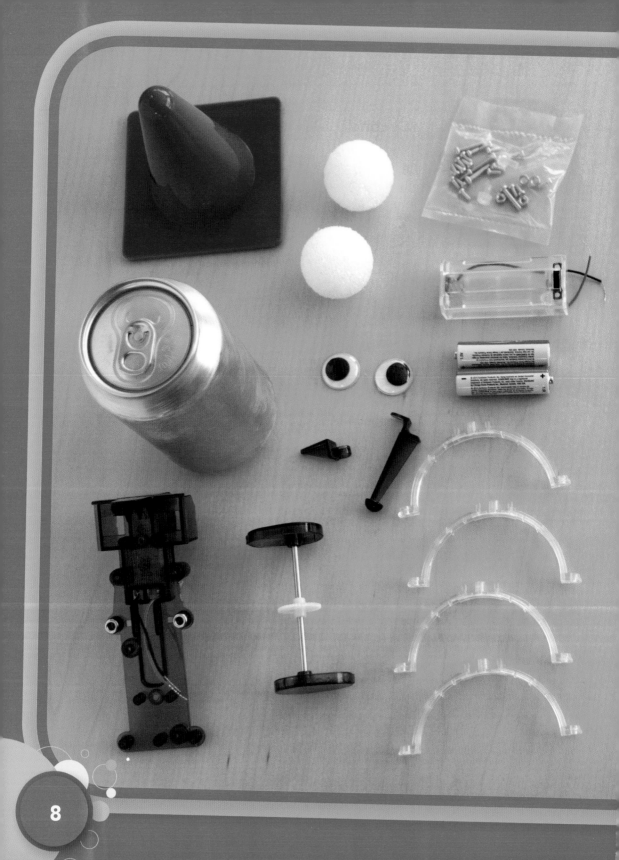

Miss Lopez said the class would build robots from 3-D shapes. Students would work in teams to build the robots. Each team would build its own robot.

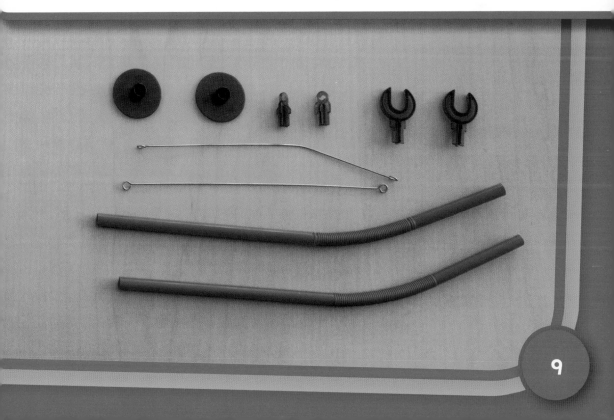

Getting Started

Teams had to think about where to use each shape. One team started with a **rectangular prism**. It would be a power pack. It would make the robot move!

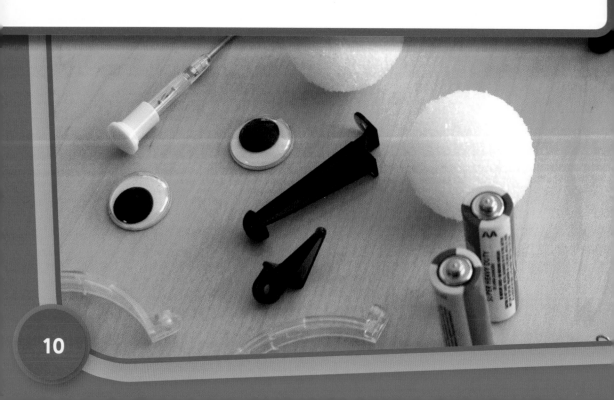

The power pack is a rectangular prism.

The can for the robot's body is a cylinder.

That team also found a good use for the **cylinder**. It would be the robot's body. They strapped it to the power pack. Then, they added the arms. Their robot was coming to life!

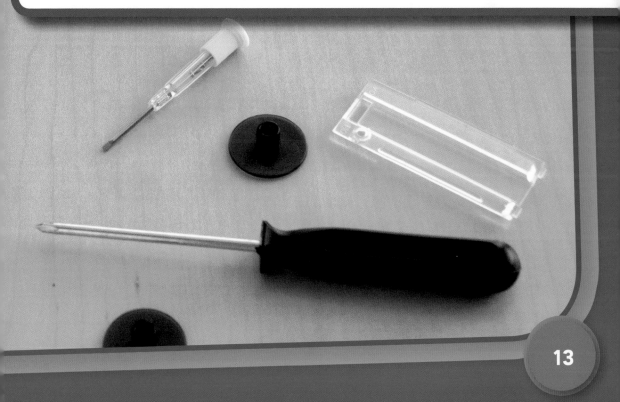

Almost Finished

The team looked at all the pieces. They tried to see which 3-D shapes were left. They made funny eyes out of **spheres**!

The eyes are two spheres.

LET'S DO MATH!

Another group wants its robot to hold an ice cream cone like this one. Choose the shapes they need.

A. B. C. D.

Last, the team wanted to find a hat for its robot. They took a cone and placed it on top. The robot was complete!

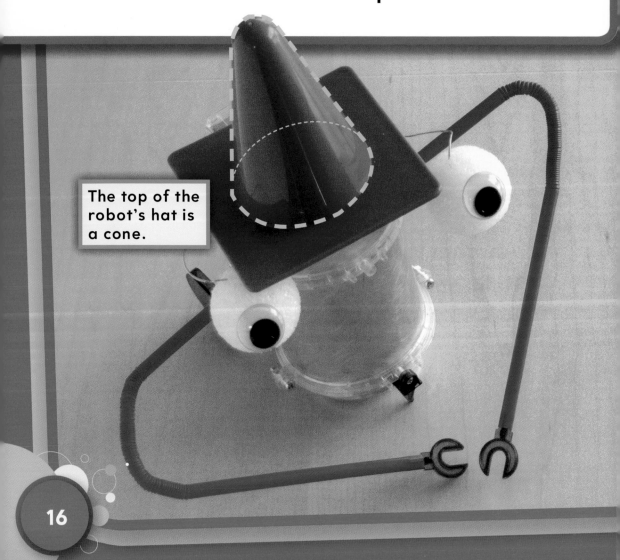

The top of the robot's hat is a cone.

Miss Lopez loves the robot hat! She builds a head and hat like this one for her robot.

1. What two shapes does Miss Lopez use to build her robot head and hat?

2. What 3-D shapes would you choose to build a robot head and hat? Why?

Proud Teacher

Miss Lopez was proud of all the teams. They had learned a lot about 3-D shapes. They had fun, too.

The class could not wait to get started on their next 3-D project!

The 3-D robot is ready to go!

⚙️ Problem Solving

Help one of Miss Lopez's robot teams design a robot. Build or draw a robot using cubes, spheres, cylinders, rectangular prisms, and cones. Complete the sentence frames to describe your robot. Then, answer the question.

1. • My robot's name is _____.

   • Its head is a _____.

   • Its eyes are _____.

   • Its body is a _____.

   • Its arms are _____.

   • Its legs are _____.

2. Compare your robot to the one on page 21. How are they alike? How are they different?

3-D Robot Builder

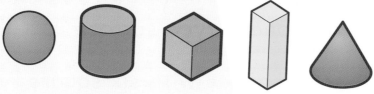

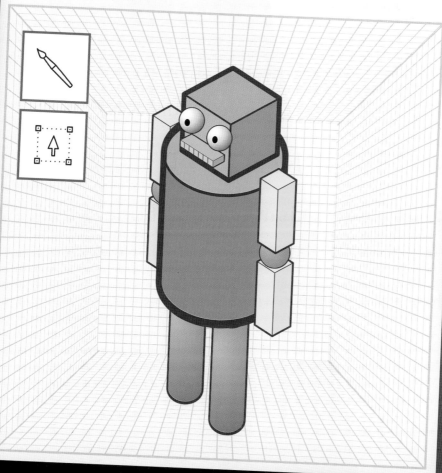

Glossary

cones—solid shapes with flat, circular bases and one curved surface

cubes—solid shapes with six square faces

cylinder—solid shape with two circular bases and one curved surface

faces—flat surfaces of 3-D shapes

rectangular prism—solid shape with rectangular faces

spheres—solid round shapes

Index

Answer Key

Let's Do Math!

page 7:

1. sphere

2. cube

page 15:

A, C

page 17:

1. cylinder, rectangular prism

2. Answers will vary.

Problem Solving

1. Answers will vary.

2. Answers will vary.